MY RETIREMENT, MY WAY

A Workbook for the Newly Retired to Create Meaning, Set Goals, and Find Happiness

Veronica McCain

ZEITGEIST · NEW YORK

Published in the United States by Zeitgeist, an imprint of Zeitgeist™, a division of Penguin Random House LLC, New York.

penguinrandomhouse.com

Zeitgeist™ is a trademark of Penguin Random House LLC

ISBN: 9780593435861
Ebook ISBN: 9780593690321

Art © Shutterstock.com/NadezhdaShu, Shutterstock.com/Kryshtofor Volodymyr, and Shutterstock.com/ VikiVector
Book design by Katy Brown
Printed in the United States of America

1 3 5 7 9 10 8 6 4 2

First Edition

For my mother, my number-one cheerleader and mentor throughout my life. Your unwavering love and belief in me have motivated me to reach for the stars.

CONTENTS

INTRODUCTION

You did it! You ran the work marathon, crossed the finish line, and received your grand trophy: *retirement*. Family and friends celebrated your glorious victory. What an accomplishment. Congratulations!

Retirement is one of the biggest transitions in life. I recall counting down the days to my own retirement and how excited I was to cross out each day on my calendar. At my retirement celebration, I almost lost it when it was time for me to speak as I saw the faces of people who were not just my coworkers but my work family. When I closed my office door for the final time, a flood of emotions came over me. This was the end of this chapter in my life. My work, which had been a significant part of my daily life for thirty-two years, was no more.

You may have experienced similar feelings when you retired. Embrace the gamut of emotions you're feeling as you begin this new chapter of your life. You have a blank slate to create the life you want, and the future is filled with vast possibilities.

You may be dealing with a flood of questions right now: *Am I going to be busy enough? What's my new purpose? Where am I going to live? Have I saved enough?* The list goes on and on. Figuring out the answers to these types of questions can feel overwhelming at times. Whether you are semi-retired or fully retired, putting together a thoughtful plan early on is key to a successful retirement. That's why I wrote this workbook—to help guide you through your first year of retirement.

This workbook includes a variety of exercises on different retirement topics. You'll encounter many thought-provoking questions throughout these pages, some of which you may not have considered yet. Your answers will help you formulate your road map to a fulfilling retirement. In addition to the exercises, you'll find information and tips to help you make the most of your retirement years.

You don't need to complete this workbook right away. Find a quiet space where you can focus on the topics and do the exercises. Take your time and answer honestly; there are no right or wrong answers. When you complete this workbook, you will have an exciting plan for your future. Remember, this is your time to experience life the way you want to. So let the journey begin!

PART ONE

Retirement Starts Here and Now

66 Retirement is not the end of the road.
It is the beginning of an open highway. 99
—Unknown

Transitioning from work to retirement is an interesting dynamic. Until now, you had something of a life road map to follow. You went to school, got a job and/or built a career, perhaps got married and raised children, and enjoyed life along the way. When you retire, the way ahead may not be as clear. You will have to design a new road map for your life from scratch. Depending on your outlook, this can be exciting or challenging—or both. Either way, retirement is not a time to sit around and wait for life to happen. Retirement is when you make life happen. Remember, you've worked most of your life to have this freedom. Be adventurous and explore new things. Don't squander your time by staying neutral.

There are no parameters around how your retirement road map should look. The road is wide open, and you can take any direction. If you make a few wrong turns, that's okay; it makes the ride more adventurous. Put the pedal to the metal and ride it out until you can't go anymore. For me, that's the best kind of road trip! This part of the book will start you on your way.

Chapter 1

WHERE ARE YOU NOW?

Susan could not wait to retire. She envisioned just taking it easy and enjoying life. When I met her six months into retirement and asked her how life was, Susan responded, "Not as I thought." She found that most of her days were long, and the stillness in her house was beginning to weigh on her during the day. Susan revealed that, to her surprise, she felt lost without her job. She told me that she had cherished the time at home when she was working, but now that she was retired, she looked for reasons to get out of the house.

That's not surprising. Our jobs not only account for our identity but also consume a lot of our time. A big void needs to be filled in retirement, but it should not be filled just with things to keep you busy. Eventually, that will be unfulfilling, and you will still start to feel a sense of emptiness. You don't want to mope around struggling to fill your days with activities. The key is to find interests and endeavors that will fulfill you. You want to wake up each morning feeling energized about what is happening in your life.

WHO ARE YOU?

Love it or hate it, your work has shaped who you currently are. It may have made you feel valued and needed—or maybe the steady paycheck gave you peace of mind. Whatever your career provided, it is no longer the source of that feeling or need. Now you must discover new reasons to get up each morning. The exercises in this section will help you reflect on your past and present so you can better understand yourself and start shaping your retirement future.

Discovering Your New Identity

To help you discover your new identity as a retired person, consider these tips:

> Schedule activities you enjoyed doing when you took time off from work.

> Journal and reflect on your expectations of yourself as a retired person.

> Read books and articles and listen to podcasts on a variety of topics to discover what most interests you now.

> Volunteer for different organizations to discover how you most enjoy helping out.

Your Retirement Outlook

Be honest with yourself about your retirement outlook and how accepting you are of this new chapter in your life. On a scale of 1 to 5, circle the number of the descriptor that best represents your feelings about retirement.

1	**2**	**3**	**4**	**5**
DIDN'T WANT TO	ANXIOUS	NEUTRAL	GOOD	ECSTATIC

If you didn't choose 4 or 5, list five steps you can take to improve your outlook:

1. _____

2. _____

3. _____

4. _____

5. _____

Were You Ready?

There are many elements to retirement life, and understanding how prepared you were when you took the leap will help you better design your road map moving forward. Check either "yes" or "no" for each statement. Even if you choose "no" for all or some, doing the exercises in this workbook can help you turn that "no" into a "yes."

	Yes	No
I have an identity and purpose outside of my job.		
I have a sound retirement financial plan.		
I have a social network that's not tied to my job.		
My family relationships are good.		
I like the lifestyle where I am living.		
I have a vision for my retirement life.		
I have passions and hobbies.		
When I set goals, I achieve them.		
I have activities that keep me busy.		
I am in good physical and mental health.		

Reflect on Your Career

Take some time to reflect on what the past decades have meant to you professionally. Whether the road was bumpy at times or mostly smooth sailing, your experiences helped shaped who you are now. Consider your answers to the following prompts and think about the impact they have on you as a newly retired person.

What is the biggest lesson you learned on the job?

_____

_____

_____

_____

What was your greatest professional accomplishment?

_____

_____

_____

_____

What or who inspired you the most and why?

_____

_____

_____

_____

What Do You Do?

When you worked and someone asked you, "What do you do?" you probably talked about your job. Now that you are retired, do you know what you will say when someone asks you that question? Your answer may change over time, but for now, write a response you would feel comfortable giving today.

_____

_____

_____

_____

_____

_____

_____

_____

_____

Reinvent What Brought You Joy

What you did for work can provide a starting point for understanding what avenues you may want to pursue now that you're retired. If you enjoyed your job, reinventing it to fit your retirement life can be an *aha* moment. For example, if you loved being a teacher, perhaps you could tutor students after school. If you were an accountant who liked working with numbers, maybe a local nonprofit needs help with its books. So think back over your life:

What brought you joy in the work you did, even if it was just a small part of your job?

_____

_____

_____

How can you reinvent this task to fit your retirement life?

_____

_____

_____

List three steps you can take to pursue this source of joy:

1. _____

2. _____

3. _____

Take an Inventory

You spent years working and developing skills and acquiring knowledge. Taking an inventory can help you figure out how you might work your skills and knowledge into your retirement—whether that's through volunteering, starting a side hustle, joining a group, trying a new hobby, or something else.

	Skills and Knowledge	How I Might Apply This in Retirement:
What work-related tasks were you best at?	1.	
	2.	
	3.	
What came naturally to you?	1.	
	2.	
	3.	
What are your strongest skills?	1.	
	2.	
	3.	
What tasks/duties, if any, were you the "go-to" person for?	1.	
	2.	
	3.	
What type of knowledge did you gain that might benefit others?	1.	
	2.	
	3.	

Have a Conversation with Family and Friends

Others may see talent and strengths in you that you have overlooked or have not even considered. Talking with friends, family, and even former coworkers about what they see as your strengths may give you good ideas about retirement possibilities. In fact, that's how I got into coaching: family and friends told me I had a knack for relating to people and inspiring them.

Have a conversation with at least three people who know you well. Give them a heads-up on the topic. Have a notepad with you to jot down their responses to these questions:

- What do you see as my strengths?
- What do you think I am talented at doing?

Now respond to these prompts:

What strengths and talents did they identify?

Are you interested in incorporating any of these strengths and talents into your retirement? If so, how?

Explore Fun Activities

The need to make a living sometimes prevents us from doing the fun things we want to do or enjoyed doing as children. Now that you're retired, you can revisit some of what you've missed out on.

What did you enjoy doing as a child?

_____

_____

_____

_____

What activities do you enjoy as an adult but have not had the time or opportunity to explore?

_____

_____

_____

_____

List three fun activities you would like to do during retirement:

1. _____

2. _____

3. _____

What Do You Miss?

The transition from work to retirement is not an on/off switch. When you retire, you do not automatically forget about work and switch to retirement mode. There will be pieces you miss about it. Reflect on what brought you joy in your work environment, unrelated to your everyday tasks. Try to think of at least three things. Maybe it was getting coffee in the cafeteria with your coworkers every morning, having your own office, or enjoying the alone time during your commute. This exercise can help you identify what is important to you and how to find ways to fill that need in retirement.

What I Miss	Why I Miss It	What Might Fill That Need

Your Roles

Over the course of a lifetime, people play many different roles, sometimes all at the same time—for example: child, student, partner/spouse, parent, sibling, boss, employee, volunteer, coach, teacher, neighbor, politician, and so on. Now that you are retired, think of six roles you would like to have moving forward and fill them in here.

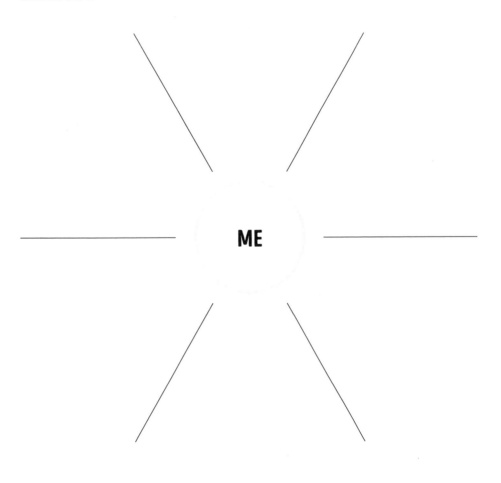

WHAT IS SUCCESS?

Before retirement, success is often defined by one's position, salary, expertise, and knowledge. These qualities may have played a significant part in helping you feel successful in life. Now that you are retired, your job will no longer determine how successful you are. You will need to view success differently. Think of it as a journey that evolves over time. What will success mean in this new journey? What will be your new expectations for feeling accomplished? The exercises in this section will help guide your transition from work success to retirement success.

Consider Consulting a Professional

If you are really struggling with the transition beyond this workbook and need help figuring out how to make your retirement successful, consider consulting with a therapist or coach. Feeling lost and uninspired is not a great way to begin this phase of your life. In any scenario, these feelings could lead to depression. Some of the most successful people seek assistance to accomplish their goals, and you can too. Professionals can help guide you to a successful retirement.

Your Definition of Success

Your definition of success should be as distinctive as you are. There are all kinds of beliefs about success that focus on jobs, money, power, looks, and so on. Your personal success, however, is not based on other people's views or beliefs. Spend 10 minutes thinking about how you define success in general, considering all your strengths, interests, and beliefs.

Define success in your own words:

_____

_____

_____

_____

How will this definition play out in your retirement?

_____

_____

_____

_____

Talk to Successful Retirees

How we perceive situations is closely tied to our experiences and observations. When we are around positive people, we tend to be more positive. Retirement is a new situation for you; your perception has probably been influenced by what you have read and seen.

Identify three retired people you know who seem to be having a successful retirement. Plan to chat with them about this topic. When you do, ask them what they have done to achieve success. Have a notepad handy so you can jot down important information.

List three key takeaways from your talks:

1. _____

_____

_____

2. _____

_____

_____

3. _____

_____

_____

Tap into Your Sense of Accomplishment

Recall how you felt when you embarked on accomplishing something important. You were motivated as you worked toward your goal, happy as you began to progress, and confident when you achieved the result. Over your lifetime, you've likely had many professional or personal accomplishments. These achievements have brought you to where you are now.

What has made you feel successful in the past?

_____

_____

_____

_____

_____

What do you want to achieve in your retirement life to feel that same sense of accomplishment?

_____

_____

_____

_____

_____

New Focal Points for Accomplishments

Now that you are retired, work is no longer the focal point for your life accomplishments. If your job played an important role in making you feel successful, you need new focal points. Here are some important considerations regarding your work-related accomplishments:

Job title/position: Without the status of your job title/position, how can you still feel relevant?

_____

_____

_____

_____

Feeling valued: Knowing that someone else is doing the job for which you were once valued, what can you do to feel valued in your retirement?

_____

_____

_____

_____

Being productive: How will you feel productive without predetermined work-related tasks?

_____

_____

_____

_____

Don't Be Afraid to Say No

You may have a hard time saying no to people who ask you to help out because you have free time as a retired person. If others impose on your time by asking you to assist with tasks and activities you don't want to do, you need to weigh whether these requests are getting in the way of what you want to accomplish. Don't deter your success by living your retirement life for others. Use this table to determine when to say a firm no.

What I Want to Accomplish	Other Person's Request	Will This Request Interfere with My Goals?	
		yes	no
		yes	no
		yes	no
		yes	no
		yes	no

Ignite the Spark

Are you a naturally curious person? When you are curious, you ignite a spark that helps you engage in new activities that are meaningful to you. Be open to learning new things—it helps boost your brainpower. On a scale of 1 to 5, rank your curiosity mindset for each statement.

1	2	3	4	5
STRONGLY DISAGREE	SOMEWHAT DISAGREE	NEUTRAL	SOMEWHAT AGREE	STRONGLY AGREE

I enjoy learning new things.	1 2 3 4 5
I seek out opportunities to grow as a person.	1 2 3 4 5
I like to be challenged.	1 2 3 4 5
I'm not afraid to step out of my comfort zone.	1 2 3 4 5
I like to meet new people.	1 2 3 4 5
I am not afraid to fail when trying something new.	1 2 3 4 5
I am focused when engaged in activities I like.	1 2 3 4 5
I have an inquisitive mind.	1 2 3 4 5
I'm not afraid to take a risk.	1 2 3 4 5
TOTAL SCORE	

Usually, the higher your total score, the more curious you are.
How would you assess your overall curiosity level?

Low   Medium   High

Are you more curious in certain scenarios than others? For example, are you curious about people and love meeting them, but when it comes to risk-taking, you'd rather play it safe? Review your rating for each statement and describe your curiosity mindset in different areas:

_____

_____

_____

_____

_____

_____

_____

_____

If your curiosity level is low overall, list three steps you can take to increase your willingness to explore new things:

1. _____

2. _____

3. _____

Think "Success"

What does success look like to you in various areas of your life? What would make you feel successful in the five common areas in this exercise? Come up with one successful thought for each area. Bring the thought to mind often to keep yourself focused on a successful retirement. For example, in the lifestyle area, a successful thought might be, "I eat a healthy diet and avoid refined sugar"; in the area of finances, one might be, "I review my spending habits monthly and make adjustments as needed."

	Successful Thought
Lifestyle	
Relationships	
Community involvement	
Personal growth	
Finances	

Key Characteristics for Success

What will success look like in your first year of retirement? Your attitude, what you aspire to, and how disciplined you are play an integral part in your overall success. Write a short sentence or phrase in each part of the pyramid describing how you will nurture these key characteristics for a successful first year of retirement.

Successful Retirement: First Year

ASPIRATION

I will achieve . . .

DISCIPLINE

I will focus my attention on . . .

ATTITUDE

I will stay positive by . . .

Chapter 2

THE NITTY-GRITTY

The financial part of retirement is a key factor to have in place, but a successful retirement is more than financial. Your social connections with family and friends and where you live also contribute to your overall well-being. You may decide to remain in your current home, or you may discover that where you lived before retirement no longer works for you. This was the case for Vanessa and Henry.

They always thought they would stay in their home until the end; however, when Vanessa retired, two years before Henry did, she soon realized that where they lived did not fit the retirement lifestyle they had envisioned. Vanessa carefully considered their retirement finances and then started looking at affordable places closer to the city, where they could easily get around and enjoy museums, theaters, restaurants, festivals, and social activities. A year after Henry retired, they sold their old home and moved closer to the city. They love their new home and all the amenities the neighborhood provides, and they've started expanding their social network.

YOUR FINANCES

Until now, your primary focus has likely been growing your retirement nest egg. In retirement, thinking shifts from accumulation to distribution. You cannot predict the future, but you can have a solid plan that gives you the confidence to handle unexpected financial situations. The golden rule when you start developing your financial retirement plan is to know your numbers: how much you will need, how much you should receive, and what your retirement investments need to achieve. The exercises in this section will help you ensure that your plan is comprehensive and based on your desired retirement lifestyle.

Cut Costs

Your retirement savings need to outlast you. Cutting costs now decreases the impact on your retirement income and life savings. Here are some tips:

> Be a conscientious traveler. Look for deals and travel in the off-season when prices are lower than peak seasons and holidays. Set a travel budget and track your expenditures.

> If you have two vehicles but only need one, sell one to save on maintenance and insurance costs.

> Evaluate your life insurance policies to see if they are still necessary or can be adjusted.

> Medical costs are one of the most significant expenses in retirement. Take commonsense steps to stay healthy.

Bring Financial Concerns to Light

Now that you are spending down your nest egg, you may worry about running out of money. Bring your concerns to light so you can start finding solutions.

How do you feel about your financial outlook in retirement?

_____

_____

_____

_____

How do you feel about spending your retirement savings?

_____

_____

_____

_____

If you have concerns, what four steps can you take to ease your mind?

1. _____

2. _____

3. _____

4. _____

Make Sound Financial Decisions

Now that it is time to spend your nest egg, you need to be sure you are making sound financial decisions. Whether you are working with a professional financial planner or are a DIY retiree, you should have some general knowledge to make wise decisions.

Check either "yes" or "no" for each statement. If you choose "no" for all or some, educate yourself on the topic to turn that "no" into a "yes." These statements are not all-inclusive but do cover some basic retirement financial knowledge.

	Yes	No
Are you able to develop a comprehensive retirement budget?		
Do you know your sources of retirement income and options?		
Do you know the best time to take social security and why?		
Do you understand how taxes affect your retirement account(s) when withdrawing money?		
Do you know how to factor inflation into your retirement budget?		
Do you understand investment risk and longevity planning?		
Do you know how to develop a sound withdrawal strategy from investments?		
Do you have a plan for required minimum distributions?		
Do you understand Medicare and which plan is best for you?		
Do you know if you should consider long-term care?		
Do you know how to develop an estate plan?		

Identify Retirement Income Sources

You used to receive a paycheck to cover your expenses; now that you are retired, you need to pay expenses from your retirement income, which is likely to come from various sources. This table helps you identify your sources of retirement income.

Income Type	Yearly Amount*	Monthly Amount*
GUARANTEED INCOME		
Social security		
Pension		
Annuity		
Other:		
RETIREMENT ACCOUNTS		
401(k)/403(b)		
Thrift Savings Plan		
IRA		
Roth IRA		
Other:		
OTHER INCOME		
Part-time work		
Rental income		
Other:		
Other:		
TOTAL INCOME:		

*Excluding taxes

Track Your Expenses

Guesstimating a certain percentage of your retirement income to pay expenses is not ideal for determining your retirement budget. Instead, track your expenses to develop an accurate budget. Start now by completing this table to get a more comprehensive view of your monthly and yearly expenses.

Expense	Monthly Amount	Yearly Amount
HOUSING		
Mortgage/rent		
Property taxes and insurance		
Repairs and maintenance		
Association dues		
UTILITIES		
Electricity		
Gas		
Water		
Phone(s)		
Internet		
Cable		
Trash collection		
FOOD		
Groceries		
Restaurants		

continued

Expense	Monthly Amount	Yearly Amount
TRANSPORTATION		
Car repairs and maintenance		
License and taxes		
Gas		
Other:		
MEDICAL		
Medications		
Doctor(s)		
Dentist		
INSURANCE		
Life insurance		
Health insurance		
Homeowner's insurance		
Auto insurance		
Long-term care insurance		
CHARITY		
Tithes		
Charity and offerings		
SAVINGS		
Emergency fund		
DEBT		
Car payment(s)		
Credit card(s)		
Student loan(s)		

continued

Expense	Monthly Amount	Yearly Amount
PERSONAL CARE		
Hair and nails		
Toiletries		
Other		
CLOTHING		
Clothing and shoes		
Accessories		
RECREATION		
Entertainment		
Vacation		
OTHER		
Subscriptions/books		
Organization dues		
Gifts		
Childcare/parent care		
Pocket money		
Technology		
Other:		
Other:		
Other:		
Other:		
TOTAL EXPENSES:		

Be a Conscientious Spender

After spending a good chunk of your lifetime building a retirement nest egg, you will want to avoid wasting your money on unimportant things. It's time to prioritize your discretionary spending. This will help you ensure that your purchases focus on items and experiences that support your retirement vision and passions.

In order of importance, what five things are necessary for you to spend discretionary money on?

1. _____

2. _____

3. _____

4. _____

5. _____

For each expenditure, explain how it does (or does not) support your vision for retirement:

1. _____

2. _____

3. _____

4. _____

5. _____

Outstanding Debt

Use this table to get clear on your outstanding debt so you can plan to eliminate or reduce it to make the most of your retirement dollars moving forward.

Type of Debt	Balance	Estimated Pay-Off Date
Mortgage		
Car loan(s)		
Student loan(s)		
Credit card(s)		
Other loan(s)		
Other:		
Other:		

What's on the Horizon?

It is hard to predict what major expenses might occur in the future that might impact your retirement budget. However, if there are situations you know are on the horizon, identify them now so you can prepare. Here are some common ones:

Change in living situation: Will your expenses increase or decrease? How will you plan for an increase?

_____

_____

_____

Medical insurance: How will the cost of medical insurance change once you retire and are eligible for Medicare?

_____

_____

_____

Long-term care: What is your plan if you need long-term care? What is the cost of long-term care insurance?

_____

_____

_____

Dependents: Does/will anyone else rely on your retirement income, and to what extent?

_____

_____

_____

Activity level: How will your expenses fluctuate over the course of your retirement based on your activity level?

_____

_____

_____

Hobbies and interests: Will any leisure activities you want to pursue result in a significant expense? How much?

_____

_____

_____

Other significant costs: Will you plan trips, make big-ticket purchases, or host any milestone celebrations? What's your plan?

_____

_____

_____

YOUR HOME

Before retirement, you may have based where you live on the proximity to work, a good school system, or your social community. Retirement is an opportunity to take a fresh look at your living arrangements. Would you like more cultural/learning opportunities? Do you want good health care facilities nearby? How will your living arrangements support your needs? Above all, your home should provide a sense of comfort, well-being, and potential for social connections. The exercises in this section will help you explore options that support your desired retirement lifestyle.

Adventurous Living Arrangements

Have you thought outside the box when it comes to your living situation? Are you looking for a big adventure in retirement? Many new retirees look for exciting ways to live this part of their lives. Some of the more common but unusual living arrangements include:

> Traveling the country in an RV

> Living year-round on cruise ships

> Living onboard a boat

> Moving abroad

> House swapping

If one of these ideas appeals to you, explore your options, take the leap that makes the most sense for you, and then . . . *live it up!*

Housing Expense Questionnaire

Housing expenses represent a large part of your retirement budget. Even if your mortgage is paid off, the cost of maintaining a house can be significant. Here are some general housing expense questions to consider.

	Yes	No
Does the mortgage/rent fit within your retirement budget?		
Have you planned for increased property taxes?		
Have you planned for increased utility expenses?		
Are the interior and exterior of your house in reasonably good condition?		
Are all your appliances in good working order?		
Does your retirement budget include a plan for major repair costs, such as a new roof?		

If you answered "no" to any of these questions, can you take steps to turn them into a "yes"? If not, what are your plans? How would downsizing or making other changes affect your housing costs?

_____

_____

_____

_____

_____

_____

How Is Your Living Situation?

Where you live should support the kind of retirement you envision and enhance your quality of life. Think about your current living situation and answer "true" or "false" for each statement.

	True	False
I am happy where I live.		
I feel safe where I am living as I age.		
My home is close to family and friends.		
I have access to culture and leisure activities that interest me.		
I have transportation options.		
I live near good medical facilities.		

If you answered "false" to any of these questions, is this matter important enough for you to change your living situation? If so, what actions will you take?

_____

_____

_____

_____

_____

_____

Assess Your Current Home

You may prefer to stay in your current home until the end. If you currently live in your forever home, assess whether it will continue to work for you as you age. Here are some basic questions to determine if you will need to make renovations when you reach the later stages of your golden years.

	Yes	No	Possible Renovation Notes
Do you have to climb steps to enter your home?			1.
			2.
			3.
Does your home have one or more staircases?			1.
			2.
			3.
Does your home have a bedroom on the first floor?			1.
			2.
			3.
Does your home have a walk-in shower with grip bars on the first floor?			1.
			2.
			3.
Are kitchen appliances and cabinets easy to reach?			1.
			2.
			3.
Can the doorways accommodate a walker or wheelchair?			1.
			2.
			3.

Making a Move

Many retirees have dreamed about relocating to a new area, and the time has come to make it happen. The excitement of making a move can easily over-shadow the reality of this major change. Doing a trial run for a few months or so in the new area can help ensure that the move is right for you. Be sure to think it through to avoid regret later. Answer these questions to get started.

Why do you want to move to this area?

Will the cost of living be more, less, or the same? If different, by how much?

Do you have social connections in this area? If not, what is your plan to develop them?

How does the new area compare to where you are living now? Does it include things you like about where you are currently living?

_____

_____

_____

_____

_____

Does this area have all the amenities and services you will need (health care, culture, leisure activities, transportation, shopping centers)? What's missing, if anything?

_____

_____

_____

_____

_____

_____

YOUR SOCIAL NETWORK

Having an active social life in retirement is essential to your overall well-being. If most of your social connections were tied to work, you may find it more challenging to make new ones. Though you may feel apprehensive at first, connecting with others who share your interests can be rewarding. When developing new friendships, try to broaden your social circle with people in all different age groups for a wider perspective on life. The exercises in this section will help you examine and widen your social network to keep unhealthy feelings of loneliness and isolation away.

Who Are Your Friends?

Friendships are essential to a happy retirement. Yours are likely grouped into close friends, good friends, and casual acquaintances. Each type of friendship comes with its own level of connection and boundaries. The deep level of support and trust you share with your close friends is different from just enjoying the company of good friends or casual acquaintances. Think about where your friends fall on this spectrum to navigate their role in your retirement life.

Is There a Place for Work Friends?

You spent a lot of time at work, so it is natural that you may have one or more strong work-related social connections. Now that you are retired, you may discover that these connections revolved mostly around what was happening at work. Over time, what's going on at your former workplace will probably no longer interest you. If you want to maintain relationships with your work friends, consider these questions for each one:

What common interests do you share outside of work?

_____

_____

_____

_____

_____

_____

How will you stay connected, and what steps will you take to make this happen?

_____

_____

_____

_____

_____

_____

Stay in Touch with True Friends

True friendships are hard to find. Be careful not to neglect them by socializing with casual acquaintances too frequently. Newly retired people often find themselves saying yes to various social gatherings just to fill up their days. Be mindful of who is grabbing your attention and whether time with those people is fulfilling or just keeping you busy. Identify your true friends, how often you will connect, and how you will stay connected to make sure you keep in touch with them in retirement.

True Friends	How Often I Will Connect	How I Will Stay Connected

Rate Your Friendship Effort

Begin your retirement by putting effort into forming lasting bonds with your friends. Friendships are shared relationships; you get out of them what you put in. On a scale of 1 to 5, rank your effort for each statement.

1	**2**	**3**	**4**	**5**
NEVER	RARELY	SOMETIMES	FREQUENTLY	ALL THE TIME

I help my friends through difficult times.	1 2 3 4 5
I am honest with my friends.	1 2 3 4 5
I am open to my friends' views and opinions.	1 2 3 4 5
I listen to my friends without interrupting.	1 2 3 4 5
I encourage and support my friends.	1 2 3 4 5
I laugh with my friends.	1 2 3 4 5
I show gratitude to my friends.	1 2 3 4 5
I am a reliable friend.	1 2 3 4 5

For any statements with low ratings, how can you improve in that area?

Discuss your ratings with one or two of your closest friends. Do they agree or disagree with your ratings? If they disagree, discuss ways to improve that area of your friendship. The goal here is to build a stronger bond, not tear it down, so be open-minded when you hear their feedback.

Explore Diversity

Avoid limiting your social circle to only those in your age group or who are just like you. Seek out friendships with people of various ages as well as those who have different interests and ideas. These friendships can keep your mind nimble, help you expand your horizons, give you different perspectives on life, and prevent you from growing lonely as you age.

To assess the diversity of your social connections, ask yourself:

- Do my friends vary in age?
- Do my friends have different interests than I do?
- Do my friends stimulate my mind?

If you answered no to any of these questions, list five ways to meet new potential friends and diversify your friendships:

1. _____

_____

2. _____

_____

3. _____

_____

4. _____

_____

5. _____

_____

Join Clubs or Groups

The thought of getting out there and starting new friendships may feel intimidating. The easiest way to meet people is to join clubs or groups. Club and group members are there precisely because they are eager to meet people who share a common interest or goal.

Name two to four activities you enjoy doing.

_____

_____

_____

_____

_____

_____

What clubs or groups in your area support these activities?

_____

_____

_____

_____

_____

_____

Reconnect with Old Friends

Now that you are no longer working, you have more time to invest in friendships. You may want to reconnect with old friends you lost contact with during your working years. This is a terrific way to build your social circle, and social media platforms make it easier to reconnect than ever before.

Think about your childhood friends, college friends, former coworkers, or previous neighborhood friends. List a few people you would like to be back in touch with and how you will reach out.

Old Friend	How and When I Will Reach Out

Your Social Calendar

You may have spent so much time focusing on your career and family that you had little time to build an active social life. Now that you have the time, start by being intentional and committed to getting out there. For the next three months, schedule three or four social activities and write them in this social calendar.

Social Activities Plan

Month 1	Date:	Activity:
	Time:	
	Date:	Activity:
	Time:	
	Date:	Activity:
	Time:	
Month 2	Date:	Activity:
	Time:	
	Date:	Activity:
	Time:	
	Date:	Activity:
	Time:	
Month 3	Date:	Activity:
	Time:	
	Date:	Activity:
	Time:	
	Date:	Activity:
	Time:	

YOUR FAMILY

Retirement often changes family dynamics. Your vision of family life may not be the reality now. For example, if you are married, you may discover that spending more time with your spouse is not quite the happily-ever-after you imagined. As you transition to retirement, consider how your family life is being impacted. How do your loved ones—perhaps a spouse, children, grandchildren, or extended family—factor into your retired life? The exercises in this section will look at your family's role in your retirement and help you strengthen your family bonds.

Nurture Your Bonds

Families with strong emotional bonds express their love for each other and take time to be together. Even if you know your family members will be there when you need them, you must still actively nurture the bond. These tips can help you keep that bond strong:

> Invite family members over for a regular game night or dinner.

> Plan family trips and/or reunions.

> Express your love and appreciation with phone calls, cards, and letters.

> Host celebrations and/or be present for special occasions.

> Offer to help with caregiving.

Your Relationship with Your Partner

Not all retirees are married, of course, but if you are, or if you have a significant other, it's important to be aware of how your relationship with your partner may change as you adjust to your new normal. It's essential to keep the lines of communication open. For this activity, sit down with your partner and discuss how you see your life together in retirement.

1. Share your retirement visions.
2. If your visions include travel, discuss how each of you feels about traveling.
3. Do you support each other's vision? If not, why not?
4. How will a lack of support impact your retirement life together? Discuss what actions you can take to align your visions. Compromising? Coaching? Counseling?
5. Discuss how much time you will spend together in retirement.
6. Discuss how much time you will spend apart while pursuing your own interests.
7. If you are not aligned on how much time you will spend together, discuss what actions you can take to align your expectations. Compromising? Coaching? Counseling?
8. If you are retiring before your partner, how will you spend your free time while they are working?
9. Discuss how household roles may change.
10. Discuss any financial adjustments you will need to make.

List five key takeaways from this discussion:

1. _____

2. _____

3. _____

4. _____

5. _____

Reconnect with Your Partner

When work is not consuming your day and you have the opportunity to spend more time with your partner or other loved one, you may find that your connection is not as strong as it once was. Instead of letting retirement drive you further apart, this is a great time to reconnect on another level.

What interests and/or hobbies do you share?

_____

_____

_____

_____

What can you do together to reach a new goal or accomplish something?

_____

_____

_____

_____

What social activities can you do together that you'll both find engaging?

_____

_____

_____

_____

Spending Time with Children

Now that you are retired, you may want to spend more time with the children in your life. Perhaps these are your adult children and grandchildren, or maybe nieces and nephews and their kids. Be aware that they are likely all leading busy lives with scheduled commitments and routines. To avoid hurt feelings and conflict, make sure that you are all aligned on how much time you will spend together.

Talk with the adults and kids about the frequency and amount of time you would like to spend with them. Are you aligned or misaligned? If misaligned, what are their expectations?

_____

_____

_____

Can you spend time with the kids without altering their routines—for example, by attending sporting activities or engaging in shared interests?

_____

_____

_____

Are you expected to help with caregiving and babysitting? If so, do you agree with these expectations? If not, what might be a good compromise?

_____

_____

_____

When Kids Come Home

It's not uncommon for adult children (boomerang kids) to move back home just when their parents retire. Having lived independently, they may return home for economic reasons. This situation can cause havoc on your retirement plan if it is not handled properly. To alleviate a stressful family relationship that can dampen your early retirement excitement, be transparent with your adult children about how their move back home will impact the family.

How will your child moving back affect your retirement plan, and how will you adjust?

_____

_____

_____

_____

_____

_____

Ask your child how long they plan to stay and what their goals are for living independently again. Take notes here:

_____

_____

_____

_____

Discuss the house rules with your child. Take notes here on the rules and your child's willingness to follow them:

_____

_____

_____

_____

_____

Discuss your child's household responsibilities and financial contributions. Take notes here on your child's willingness and ability to meet these expectations:

_____

_____

_____

_____

_____

What will you do if things don't go according to plan? How will it impact you? Prepare for this scenario now and have a plan in place.

_____

_____

_____

_____

_____

Moving Closer

When you retire, you may want to move closer to the younger generation(s) in your family; this can help provide feelings of comfort and support. In addition, being close to the little ones allows you to see them grow up while being an integral part of their lives. These are all great reasons to move closer, but be sure to think it through first.

Respond "yes" or "no" to each of the following statements. For any "no" answer, determine if there's anything that can turn that "no" into a "yes." Taking all your answers into account, decide if moving closer to family is a good choice.

	Yes	No
I can afford to relocate.		
I can afford the cost of living on my retirement budget.		
The children want me to move closer.		
I would want to live in the area even if the children didn't live there.		
They plan on staying in the area for a while.		
The possibility that they will have to relocate for a job is slight.		
I have a plan if they relocate.		
I have social connections in the area outside of my family.		
I am comfortable with the health care facilities in the area.		
The area has resources that fit my desired lifestyle.		

Stay Connected

Staying connected to all your family members is important throughout the retirement years. This means more than just staying in touch through texting and social media. When you are newly retired, you need to nurture your family relationships from the get-go; don't wait until you need them.

In this diagram, write a statement for each of the five categories stating how you will stay connected.

PARENTS

_____

_____

GRANDCHILDREN   EXTENDED FAMILY

_____

_____

MY
FAMILY

_____

_____

SIBLINGS   CHILDREN

_____

_____

_____

Consider Your Aging Parents

When you first retire, you may be lucky enough to have parents who are still strong and vital. As they age, however, they may need your assistance and support. To avoid being caught off guard, have a basic plan in place. Discuss this plan with your parents so they feel at ease knowing you are there to support them if needed.

How do your parents want to be cared for if they need assistance?

_____

_____

_____

_____

Will you be the primary person responsible for your parents' care? If you have siblings, will they help?

_____

_____

_____

_____

What are your responsibilities with regard to your aging parents' care?

_____

_____

_____

_____

Do you or other family members who can help live near your parents?

_____

_____

_____

_____

Are elder-care services available where they live if needed?

_____

_____

_____

_____

How will caring for your parents affect your retirement, personally and/or financially?

_____

_____

_____

_____

Reconnecting with an Estranged Relative

Life is short—and it seems to get even shorter when you retire. If there is a certain family member you have been estranged from and would like to reconnect with, now is the time to make it happen. Without work and other life circumstances getting in the way, you have the opportunity to prioritize what is important to you. Fill in this page and then reach out.

Relative I would like to reconnect with:

Why I want to reconnect:

The potential impact of reconnecting:

How I will stay connected:

Chapter 3

YOUR VISION OF RETIREMENT

Tony decided he would retire in the summer. He found his work dull and uninspiring, and since his finances were in order, he felt he was ready. He had never thought, however, about how his life would unfold outside of work. When friends asked him what he planned to do when he retired, he would say, "Relax and take it easy." Six months after retiring, Tony was doing just that—sitting around the house, relaxing, and taking it easy. Occasionally, he would meet up with friends for golf and lunch, but most of his time was spent watching TV. When friends asked Tony how he was enjoying retirement, he would say, "I loathe it."

As the saying goes, "You want to retire *to* something, not *from* something." Ideally, you should begin developing your retirement vision before you set a retirement date, but it's not too late to create one now. Your retirement vision is the driving force that propels you to strive toward what you want. It is the starting point for laying out a thoughtful retirement plan so you can move forward feeling confident and excited about the possibilities.

HOPES AND FEARS

You've heard about the good life and want to experience it. You've waited for this opportunity to pursue your passions and desires and not be confined by work responsibilities. Still, you may have fears too. The most common fears in retirement are running out of money, health care costs, and aging. These are valid concerns, but don't let them paralyze you and stop you from enjoying your retirement. With careful preparation, you can put your worries to rest and focus on those amazing hopes and dreams. The exercises in this section will help you develop a retirement vision and work through your fears.

Common Fears

Many "what if" scenarios may start swirling in your head when you are newly retired. You don't really know what the future will hold as the years pass. Here are some tips for dealing with the most common retirement fears:

> Aging: Develop an exercise routine that includes mental stimulation.

> Boredom: Stay active, vibrant, and pursue your passions.

> Health care costs: Get the right insurance and create a health savings plan.

> Running out of money: Develop a realistic retirement budget plan.

Express Your Gratitude

Being able to retire is a wonderful opportunity. Don't take for granted having the resources to make this life-changing decision. Being thankful and showing gratitude helps cultivate a positive attitude. Be sure to take time to reflect on why this phase of life is so special. Think about what this next chapter means to you.

List three reasons you are grateful for retirement:

1. _____

2. _____

3. _____

Stay Optimistic

You probably have many hopes and dreams for your newly retired life. As time goes on, it is essential to stay positive and motivated. Complete these statements with words or phrases to keep yourself encouraged and optimistic about the future.

I believe my retirement is _____

_____

What matters most to me is _____

_____

I will stay vibrant in retirement by _____

_____

Develop a Brighter Outlook

Maybe you didn't have a choice about when you retired. If retirement is forced on you when you don't feel ready, it's natural to feel upset and fearful. Take some time to acknowledge your feelings, but do make an effort to move toward a brighter outlook. Holding on to negative feelings will hinder your ability to move forward. Take these steps:

1. Come up with two positive affirmations about your retirement by completing these statements:

    Now that I'm retired, I have the opportunity to

    and .

    Now that I'm retired, I will thrive because I am

    and .

2. Remind yourself of past victories to renew your faith in yourself, then jot down three actions you can take to move on to a victorious retirement life:

    Action 1:

    Action 2:

    Action 3:

3. Name three supportive people in your life who believe in your abilities to thrive despite this situation and can help you through it:

    Person 1:

    Person 2:

    Person 3:

Map Out Your Fears

There are many unknowns in retirement, which may play out in your head and keep you in a state of anxiety. To help ease your mind, map out your fears in this grid. This process will help you put your fears in perspective and motivate you to find solutions.

My Fears	Why I Have These Fears
Actions That Will Ease My Fears	**The Impact of Not Having These Fears**

If you find yourself unable to move past your fears, consider speaking to a counselor or coach.

How You Overcame Past Fears

Chances are you have encountered fearful times throughout your life that you eventually overcame. Think about your first day on a new job, a major life change, or any scenario where you needed to pursue a new avenue in life without having all the answers.

Describe a time when you feared not knowing the outcome of a new situation:

_____

_____

_____

_____

Describe the actual outcome and how you overcame your fear:

_____

_____

_____

_____

How might you use this prior experience to help you overcome your retirement fears?

_____

_____

_____

_____

Your Retirement Vision Statement

As you have been working through these pages, you've thought a lot about how you want your life to unfold—what you will be doing, what you want to accomplish, what you value, and who you will socialize with. As you continue to reflect on these concepts, summarize them into a vision statement. Use this statement to stay on track to reach your retirement goals.

Yours can be more specific, but here is a generic example: *"I embrace my retirement years by socializing with interesting people of all ages, taking classes on subjects of interest, staying connected with family, living in alignment with my values, and contributing to society."*

My Retirement Vision Statement

THINKING OF THE FUTURE

Visualize how your life will look one year or even five years from now. Take those images and use them as catalysts to start building your retirement future. What actions can you begin taking now to create the life you imagine one year from now? You don't want to come to the end of your life and regret not putting in the work to reach your goals. The exercises in this section will help you explore how your retirement life unfolds in the next few years. You will look into the future to help lay out your retirement plan now.

Cultivate a Positive Mindset

Having a positive mindset about your future is key to a successful retirement. Here are some tips to help you cultivate one:

> Learn how to let go of beliefs that hold you back.

> Quiet your mind and listen to your heart.

> Envision life unfolding the way you want it to.

> Imagine yourself achieving your goals in detail.

> Feel the feelings associated with a peaceful retirement.

> Focus on the future, not the past.

Set Goals

Ideally, you will spend many vibrant and healthy years in retirement. Newly retired, you may have all kinds of ideas about what you want to accomplish in the years ahead. Some of these goals can be accomplished in a year, but others will take longer. The best way to organize your ideas is to write down the key accomplishments you would like to achieve in one, two, and three years.

Goals for Year 1	Goals for Year 2	Goals for Year 3

Look Back from the End

Have you thought about what you would like to have accomplished by the end of your life? Thinking this way helps you solidify what is important to work on now. It also puts a lifetime in perspective (after all, we don't live forever). You need to start making plans now to achieve your end-of-life goals.

What main accomplishments do you want to have to your credit at the end of your life?

_____

_____

_____

_____

List two actions you can start taking now to make them a reality:

1. _____

2. _____

What would you like friends and family to say about the type of person you were?

_____

_____

_____

_____

List two actions you can start taking now to make this a reality:

1. _____

2. _____

Visualize Your Ideal Self

Visualization is a technique that may help you make your dreams a reality. Imagine an ideal version of yourself one year into retirement. Bring to mind all the wonderful details and look at yourself in the mirror of your mind's eye with a smile on your face. Everything is just the way you want it. In the mirror below, write down everything you observe. For example, do you look more relaxed, healthier, wiser, more self-assured?

Visualize Your Ideal Situation

Visualize your ideal situation three years from now. Close your eyes for a few minutes and bring to mind all the wonderful details. When you're ready, fill in the clouds.

WHERE ARE YOU LIVING?

WHERE HAVE YOU VISITED?

WHO IS IN YOUR SOCIAL CIRCLE?

WHAT HOBBIES AND INTERESTS DO YOU PURSUE?

WHAT HAVE YOU LEARNED?

Think for Yourself

When you begin retirement without a clear vision, you can be easily influenced by what others think you should do. Think about what you want, not what others want for you. You don't want to be living your life for others. Get in the mindset of thinking for and about yourself.

In what ways are others influencing how you live your life in retirement?

_____

_____

_____

_____

_____

What changes do you need to make to live your retirement life your way?

_____

_____

_____

_____

_____

What three steps can you take now to start making those changes?

1. _____

2. _____

3. _____

Let Go of the Past

Sometimes, envisioning the future is challenging because your mind is stuck on a past unpleasant experience. Dwelling on the past keeps you from moving forward. You can't change what has happened. To move forward, let go of what is holding you back.

What are you stuck on that happened in the past?

_____

_____

_____

_____

What lesson did you learn from that experience that can help you now?

_____

_____

_____

_____

What can you do moving forward to avoid repeating a similar experience or circumstance?

_____

_____

_____

_____

Brainstorm an Action Plan

You may have many ideas of what you want to do now that you have retired. Sometimes, however, that's where it ends—just as a thought in your head. Help turn your ideas into actions by brainstorming an action plan for each of your ideas. Use this brainstorming diagram for one idea that really excites you. You can re-create it on paper for the other things you have thought about doing.

WHY IS IT IMPORTANT?

_____

_____

_____

WHAT IS NEEDED TO MAKE IT HAPPEN?

MAIN IDEA

WHEN IS IT GOING TO HAPPEN?

_____

_____

_____

HOW IS IT GOING TO HAPPEN?

_____

_____

_____

PART TWO

Create Meaning and Find Your Passion

> " There is not one big cosmic meaning for all; there is only the meaning we each give to our life, an individual meaning, an individual plot, like an individual novel, a book for each person. " —Anaïs Nin

Sometimes the most surprising part of transitioning to retirement is realizing how much your job fulfilled you. You may not have ever thought about finding meaning and passion in your life because you found them in your job without even realizing it. Then, once you retire, it hits you—there's an empty feeling you can't describe. That's when you know you need a new focus in life. You need to feel excited about something.

Begin now to think about what a *meaningful* retirement life will involve. What are you passionate about doing? What qualities draw you toward something? Creating meaning in retirement takes a deep understanding of what you value and what holds significance for you.

Dig deep to discover what really matters to you going forward. Broaden your horizons and think beyond your own needs. How can you contribute to society in a way that makes you feel valued? Take time to reflect on your retirement pursuits. You have lived long enough to know when you feel enthusiastic about something. The chapters and exercises in this part of the book will help you develop your path to find true meaning and passion in retirement.

Chapter 4

THE MEANING OF MEANING

Retirement is essentially a blank slate. As you start filling it in, be true to your beliefs and what inspires you. Reflect on your life and identify those moments outside of work when you felt that what you were doing mattered. What you found meaning in during your preretirement years could lead to your next venture in retirement. Perhaps there is a cause you have always been interested in; maybe you volunteered for a nonprofit in your free time and now, in retirement, you want to explore that further. This was the case for Julie.

While working, Julie enjoyed volunteering at an organization that provided clothing to women and children in crisis. She even found a way to incorporate her volunteer work into her job by holding annual clothing drives at her company. When Julie retired, she became more involved with the organization, dedicating more time to helping out and mentoring some of the women. Now she serves on the board. Julie valued being able to help others, and she aligned her values with her volunteer work.

WHAT DO YOU VALUE?

Your values influence your priorities and how you will spend your time in retirement. What do you value most? Knowing your values and why they are important to you are your guideposts for the future. If your life is not aligned with your values, frustration easily arises. Recognizing and sticking to your values will help you make wiser decisions. The exercises in this section will help you identify your values and understand their importance. You will also work on ensuring that your values align with your lifestyle and retirement goals.

The Impact of Your Values

Your values drive your actions; they help motivate you and give your life meaning. Just because you've stopped working doesn't mean you've stopped growing. When you live by your values, your life will continue expanding in ways that fulfill you. Your values influence your behavior, shape your attitude, impact your decisions, determine what's important, affect how you relate to people, and create your future. Knowing your values clarifies where you are headed.

Revisit a Happy Moment

To help you discover your values, think of one of the happiest moments in your life. Bring it to mind as vividly as you can and then answer these questions:

Where were you?

_____

_____

What were you doing?

_____

_____

Who were you with?

_____

_____

What about this experience made you happy?

_____

_____

What values can you associate with that experience? For example, if a happy moment occurred during a Caribbean vacation with family, associated values might be _family_ **and** _adventure_.

_____

_____

Identify Qualities You Admire

When you admire someone, it's usually because they have a certain quality that is important to you. Follow these steps to discover qualities you wish to adopt in your retirement life:

1. Think about four people you admire and write their names in the table below.
2. List the qualities you admire about each person (for example, *kind, adventurous, intelligent,* and so on).
3. Circle any of those qualities you would like to focus on in retirement.
4. Create one or more action steps to put each quality into action.

People I Admire	Their Outstanding Qualities	Action Steps

What Do You Value?

Your values guide the decisions you make in life. As you decide what interests and activities you want to pursue in retirement, it is important to know whether they align with your values. Here's a list to get you started thinking about what you value (add to it as needed):

ACCOUNTABILITY	FUN	KNOWLEDGE
ACHIEVEMENT	GIVING	LOVE
AUTHENTICITY	GROWTH	LOYALTY
BALANCE	HAPPINESS	MOTIVATION
COMPASSION	HARD WORK	PASSION
CREATIVITY	HONESTY	PURPOSE
CURIOSITY	INSPIRING	SERVICE
DETERMINATION	INTEGRITY	SPIRITUALITY
FAIRNESS	INTELLIGENCE	THOUGHTFULNESS
FOCUS	JOY	UNITY
FRIENDSHIP	KINDNESS	

List your top 10 values and explain why they are important to you.

1. _____ is important

because _____.

2. _____ is important

because _____.

3. _____ is important

because _____ .

4. _____ is important

because _____ .

5. _____ is important

because _____ .

6. _____ is important

because _____ .

7. _____ is important

because _____ .

8. _____ is important

because _____ .

9. _____ is important

because _____ .

10. _____ is important

because _____ .

Evaluate the Impact of Values on Your Life

Living in line with your values is important to how you feel. Think about where you are now in each of the following areas in your life. On a scale of 1 to 5, evaluate how your values align in these areas.

1	**2**	**3**	**4**	**5**
NOT ALIGNED	RARELY ALIGNED	SOMEWHAT ALIGNED	ALIGNED	STRONGLY ALIGNED

Family relationships	1 2 3 4 5
Friendships	1 2 3 4 5
Physical health	1 2 3 4 5
Emotional health	1 2 3 4 5
Spiritual/faith connection	1 2 3 4 5
Leisure time/recreational activities	1 2 3 4 5
Community involvement/volunteerism	1 2 3 4 5

For any area you rated lower than 3, why do you think they aren't aligned?

_____

_____

_____

_____

List five action steps you can take to make this area more aligned with your values (use additional paper if needed for other areas):

1. _____

_____

2. _____

_____

3. _____

_____

4. _____

_____

5. _____

_____

Does Your Behavior Align with Your Values?

Now that you have a better idea of what you value, think about an average day, the activities you generally engage in weekly, and your goals for retirement life. Carefully consider the following questions:

Does your behavior align with your values? If not, what actions do you need to take to align better?

_____

_____

_____

_____

Do your values align with your retirement vision? If not, where is the disconnect, and what actions do you need to take to align better?

_____

_____

_____

_____

How will your values impact your retirement lifestyle and motivate you to create a fulfilling retirement?

_____

_____

_____

_____

Consider Your Values in Post-retirement Work

If your retirement plan includes working as a part-time employee, consultant, contractor, or entrepreneur, consider whether a potential job is in alignment with your work values. Review the list of work-related values below and rate their importance. Keep this in mind when you pursue work in retirement.

1	**2**	**3**	**4**
NOT IMPORTANT	MODERATELY IMPORTANT	IMPORTANT	VERY IMPORTANT

Rating	Value	Description
1 2 3 4	Teamwork	Working with a team toward a common goal.
1 2 3 4	Competition	Engaging in work that pits my abilities against others'.
1 2 3 4	Authority	Having the power to make my own decisions.
1 2 3 4	Leadership	Leading projects or units.
1 2 3 4	Supervision	Being responsible for work done by others.
1 2 3 4	Creativity	Creating new programs or ideas.
1 2 3 4	Recognition	Being recognized for my work.
1 2 3 4	Independence	Being able to do my work independently without significant direction.
1 2 3 4	Freedom	Being able to work on my schedule.
1 2 3 4	Connections	Having day-to-day contact with people.

Create a Core Value Statement

Write one phrase that summarizes the number-one value you will live by in retirement. This is your core value. It can be your guidepost every morning when you get out of bed. For example, if your core value is *joy*, perhaps your core value statement will be something like *"I pursue joy in all its forms."*

Core Value Statement

STAYING MOTIVATED

Before retirement, your motivation may have come naturally. In fact, you may have felt there weren't enough hours in the day to accomplish everything on your to-do list. But without the driving force to get to work, some new retirees struggle with finding the motivation to get their day started. Relying on yourself to keep the momentum going can be challenging, so you may need to learn to be more self-motivated. The exercises in this section will help you assess your motivation, discover new ways to maintain it, and avoid getting discouraged.

Journal for Motivation

Your inner voice is what pushes you forward. This is an optimal time to tune in to it. With the noise from your job gone, you will have more time to focus on your thoughts. Start journaling to discover what motivates you. As the days and weeks progress, review your journal entries for commonalities that point to what motivates you. Here are two journaling tips:

> When you wake up, capture your first thoughts of the day.

> At the end of the day, capture what you spent most of your time doing. What did you think about most during the day? What made you feel happy?

Rate Your Mindset

A positive attitude is crucial to keep you motivated, while a poor attitude can sap your energy. Figure out what mindset you are starting with so you can make an attitude adjustment if necessary to get the most out of your retirement years.

On a scale of 1 to 10, with 1 being not at all, 5 being neutral, and 10 being very much, rate each of the following statements and explore your rating.

I am looking forward to the years ahead as a retired person.

1   2   3   4   5   6   7   8   9   10

Explain your rating:

_____

_____

If your rating was low, what changes can you make to increase it?

_____

_____

I want to accomplish something meaningful in retirement.

1   2   3   4   5   6   7   8   9   10

Explain your rating:

_____

_____

If your rating was low, what changes can you make to increase it?

_____

_____

It is important to have a clear vision of what my retirement life will look like.

1   2   3   4   5   6   7   8   9   10

Explain your rating:

_____

_____

If your rating was low, what changes can you make to increase it?

_____

_____

When Were You Most Motivated?

Your past helps shape your future. Looking back over the past decades, identify an experience when you felt the most motivated, a time when you woke up excited about what was happening in your life, and explore it here.

Most motivational experience:

_____

_____

_____

_____

What about this experience made you feel motivated?

_____

_____

_____

_____

How can you create a similar experience in retirement?

_____

_____

_____

_____

Triggers That Trip You Up

Everyone has triggers that sometimes throw them off course. These triggers can be even more powerful in retirement, especially in the early days when you are trying something new. What are some of the triggers that might cause you to give up? List four triggers; for each one, identify a few ways to counteract it when it shows up.

Trigger	Ideas to Counteract the Trigger

Rate Your Motivational Traits

Knowing where you are in life with key motivational characteristics is a good starting point for understanding how and why you are motivated. Each of the following statements focuses on a motivational trait. Rate your satisfaction for each area on a scale of 1 to 5.

1	**2**	**3**	**4**	**5**
NOT SATISFIED	MODERATELY SATISFIED	NEUTRAL	SATISFIED	VERY SATISFIED

I am productive.	1 2 3 4 5
I can do things independently.	1 2 3 4 5
I have a positive attitude about myself.	1 2 3 4 5
I feel accomplished.	1 2 3 4 5
Others do not pressure me to do things.	1 2 3 4 5
I am valued/appreciated.	1 2 3 4 5
I feel connected with friends and family.	1 2 3 4 5

For any statement you rated less than 4, what steps can you take to improve your rating?

_____

_____

_____

Your Motivational Toolkit

Like your life before retirement, your life as a retired person will have its highs and lows. Without a job to get you up and going, you will need a plan for when the lows hit to keep yourself from getting too far off track.

Put together a toolkit of things you can do to pause, reflect, and then get back on track. Here are some suggestions:

- Exercise
- Garden
- Get a spa treatment
- Go to a beach/lake
- Listen to music
- Meditate
- Read an inspirational book
- Socialize
- Walk in nature

My Motivational Toolkit

_____

_____

_____

_____

_____

_____

_____

_____

Your Accountability Partner

Self-motivation can be challenging because it requires you to rely on yourself to keep life moving forward. Sometimes you may need a little encouragement. Who in your life would give you a push when you need it? Reach out to this person to see if they agree to this role, and then respond to the following:

Accountability partner: _____

Why is this person an excellent accountability partner for you?

_____

_____

_____

_____

How will they hold you accountable?

_____

_____

_____

_____

What Is Your "Why"?

If there are no consequences, it is easy to give up when situations become difficult. Your desire is strong, but your will may weaken when you are presented with an obstacle. To avoid becoming discouraged when times get tough, ask yourself, "Why am I doing this?" Your "why" is the driving force to keep you motivated. Not knowing your "why" leads to:

- All talk, no action
- Fear of failure
- Inconsistency
- Indecisiveness
- Procrastination
- Self-doubt

Name one retirement goal or task you would like to complete and describe why this is important to you:

_____

_____

_____

Is your "why" significant enough to motivate you if the goal or task becomes challenging? (If you aren't sure, think about what would happen if you didn't do it.)

_____

_____

_____

How would not completing this goal or task affect your retirement life? How would you feel?

_____

_____

_____

Your Motivational Factors

The following statements focus on aspects of your life that will help keep you motivated. For each statement, answer "true" or "false."

	True	False
I have retirement goals.		
I have a daily routine.		
I have a bucket list.		
I am passionate about my pursuits.		
I have a physically active lifestyle.		
I have a satisfying social life.		
I am planning to learn new things.		
I routinely practice gratitude and thankfulness.		

If you chose "true" for most of these statements, you are strongly motivated to make the best of your retirement years. For any statements you marked "false," how can you improve your motivation in that area? What actions can you take to turn that "false" into a "true"?

_____

_____

_____

_____

Chapter 5

DISCOVER (OR REDISCOVER) YOUR PASSION

Your first year of retirement is just the beginning of a new lifestyle. You will be freer than you have probably ever been in your adult life. You are no longer bogged down with job responsibilities and the stress or pressure that ensues. Your new freedom will allow you to spend more time doing what you love. Maybe you put a hidden desire on hold due to the demands of your job, or perhaps there is something new out there you have not discovered. Retirement is an excellent time to find your passion in life.

Jim's passion has always been traveling. When he retired, his goal was to travel around the world. However, once he retired and began traveling, Jim soon realized that his travel expenses were depleting his nest egg a little too quickly for his comfort. He didn't want to give up his passion for travel, so he needed to find a way to travel and maintain a healthy retirement investment account. Jim decided to start a small travel business. He knew people who enjoyed hearing about his travel expeditions but did not enjoy the logistics of travel planning. Jim began putting together travel tours that allowed him to travel for free while enjoying others' company. He had found a way to pursue his passion without breaking the bank.

NAME YOUR PASSIONS

A surefire way to feel fulfilled is to be passionate about whatever you are pursuing. When you are passionate about something, your energy level is high; you're motivated and happy. If you already have things you are passionate about pursuing, you are on your way to getting the most out of your retirement years. But if you need help finding your passions, get out there and explore—passion will not come knocking on your door. The exercises in this section will help you discover what you love to do.

The Benefits of Volunteering

Getting involved in community service is one of the best ways to find passionate work in retirement. You can volunteer as an individual or with a group. Volunteering is an excellent social outlet, as it helps you build connections with people in your community. It also provides mental stimulation and growth, and helps you stay active. When you find a cause that ignites your passion, you may discover that volunteering is one of the most rewarding ways to spend your retirement years.

Do What You Love

Aim to spend most of your time in retirement doing what you love the most, those tasks and activities you feel most passionate about. List five activities you love doing and explain why each brings you joy.

I Love To...	Because...

How will you incorporate these activities into your retirement life more often?

What Did You Enjoy?

Searching for and discovering your passion in retirement can be a fun adventure. Looking back to what you enjoyed during your childhood is a good starting point. This is a time when you pursued your interests with more freedom. Close your eyes and see yourself as the child you once were, and then respond to the following questions.

What activities did you enjoy participating in?

\
\
\
\
\

What were some of your interests?

\
\
\
\
\
\

What were some of your hobbies?

_____

_____

_____

_____

Have you pursued any of these activities, interests, and/or hobbies as an adult?
If so, did they take a backseat to work and other responsibilities? If you didn't
pursue them, why not?

_____

_____

_____

_____

Would you like to pursue any of these activities, interests, and/or hobbies in
retirement? If so, how can you revive them?

_____

_____

_____

_____

Fill in the Passion

If you are struggling to find your passion in retirement, complete each of the following statements with the first idea that comes to mind. You may be surprised by what you uncover!

I wonder what it would be like to _____

_____.

I want to be known for _____

_____.

I could spend all day _____

_____.

If success were guaranteed, I would _____

_____.

If money were no obstacle I would _____

_____.

I would love to learn how to _____

_____.

Go Exploring

To discover your passion, you may need to get out and explore. Don't think of this exercise as narrowing down what you are passionate about. Simply list things you would like to learn about, see, and discover. You need to be intentional here, so state how and when you will follow up within the first few years of retirement.

What I Would Like to Explore	How and When

Look All Around for Your Passion

Finding your passion is not about identifying just one thing. It is about looking at all the areas of your retirement life and finding your passion in each one. What drives you in each of these areas?

SOCIAL NETWORK

_____

_____

_____

_____

COMMUNITY

_____

_____

_____

_____

GROWTH

_____

_____

_____

_____

HEALTH

_____

_____

_____

LEISURE ACTIVITIES

_____

_____

_____

Redesign Your Work Passion

One of your passions has been the job you were performing in your area of expertise, but perhaps the demands became too much and retirement was a way to slow down. You may want to continue working in the field but not in a full-time capacity. Think about how you can redesign your work passion to fit your retirement lifestyle.

What parts of your job would you enjoy doing in retirement?

_____

_____

Write a brief job description for the position you would love to have:

_____

_____

What is your ideal work schedule to fit your retirement lifestyle?

_____

_____

What can you do to make this position a reality and who might assist you (for example, former colleagues or a life/retirement coach)?

_____

_____

A Second Career

Many retirees do not see retirement as the end of having a career but as the start of establishing a new career focused on their passion. This second career doesn't feel like a job because it's something they thoroughly enjoy doing. If you want to pursue a second career, there's much to consider:

What makes you excited about pursuing a second career?

_____

_____

_____

_____

_____

How can you leverage your skills and talents to pursue this career?

_____

_____

_____

_____

_____

If you need additional training or education, what is the first step you have to take?

_____

_____

_____

_____

_____

What is your ideal work schedule (full time, part time, flexible)?

_____

_____

_____

_____

_____

What is the most meaningful action you can take now to pursue your second career?

_____

_____

_____

_____

_____

HEAD TOWARD HAPPINESS

Everyone's retirement lifestyle is different. Some retirees enjoy being busy all the time, while others want to relax and take life as it comes. As you start pursuing your passions, how will they factor into your retirement life? Will they be part of a routine schedule or something you pursue whenever the feeling hits you? It is important to take the time to figure out how your retirement life will adjust to pursuing your passions. The key is to discover a routine that works best for you. The exercises in this section focus on getting you to that happy place.

Put a Smile on Your Face

A Japanese philosophy of happiness is called *ikigai*. It's what puts a smile on your face. Finding your *ikigai* (your "reason for being") requires deep reflection on your wants and needs. While the concept is more complex than can be described here, *ikigai* involves the overlapping of these four areas:

> What you love

> What you are good at

> What you do

> What the world needs

When these areas overlap, you find your *ikigai*—a balanced, happy life. Set about developing your *ikigai* in retirement.

How Active Do You Want to Be?

Some people need to be busy to feel happy, while others are looking for a more relaxed lifestyle and highly value their downtime. Still others want the best of both worlds.

Think about how active you want to be in these next few years. Spend a few moments visualizing yourself a year from now enjoying your desired activity level. Then describe your ideal version as if it were already your reality:

_____

_____

_____

_____

_____

_____

_____

_____

_____

_____

_____

_____

_____

Emphasize What Makes You Happy

Think about all the areas of your retirement lifestyle—from post-retirement work, family, and volunteerism to leisure activities, travel, and beyond. Which areas do you want to place the most emphasis on in the years to come? Which areas do you need to deemphasize (but not necessarily eliminate) to help you effectively pursue your passions and what makes you happy? Jot them down here and keep them in mind in the months and years to follow.

Emphasize...	Deemphasize...

Your Happiness Mindset

Are you optimistic about achieving happiness over the course of your retirement years? If you waver in your response, get clear on what might be making you feel pessimistic by exploring your answers to the following questions:

What does a happy retirement look like to you?

_____

_____

_____

Is pursuing your passions important to a happy retirement? Why or why not?

_____

_____

_____

What concerns do you have that may be interfering with a happy retirement future?

_____

_____

_____

_____

List three actions you can take to overcome your doubts:

1. _____

2. _____

3. _____

The Heart of the Matter

Retirement is about having the time to do what you love, what gives you meaning, and what makes you feel passionate. Spend a few minutes revisiting these ingredients for a happy retirement here and then brainstorm how to combine them into everything that brings a smile to your face. Record those thoughts and ideas in the heart on the following page for safekeeping.

What I love to do:

_____

_____

_____

What gives me meaning:

_____

_____

_____

What I'm passionate about:

_____

_____

_____

PART THREE

Set Goals

> "If you want to be happy, set a goal that commands your thoughts, liberates your energy, and inspires your hopes."
> —Andrew Carnegie

Throughout this workbook, you have completed numerous exercises to help you discover your interests, aspirations, and passions. You have also worked on exercises to help you maintain a healthy and balanced lifestyle in retirement. Now it's time to tie all these areas together to develop your short- and long-term goals in retirement. Your short-term goals will focus on your daily/monthly lifestyle, while your long-term goals will focus on what you want to accomplish in your first year of retirement and beyond.

Setting retirement goals helps you stay focused on what you would like to achieve. When you work toward your goals, you add structure to your days, create new habits, and implement the steps needed to achieve them. People with retirement goals are generally happier and live more fulfilling lives. Your goals will provide you with clarity, keep you motivated, and help you achieve the retirement life you truly want.

Chapter 6

SHORT-TERM GOALS

Have you thought about how you want your daily and weekly life to flow now that you are retired? Do you have a regular routine that keeps you focused and feeling excited for the new day? I have found that retirees often focus on one or two big goals, but they do not consider what daily living will be like in retirement. This was the case with Lisa.

Lisa's only goal for her early years of retirement was to travel. She wanted to see the world, so she made a bucket list of places she wanted to go. Her goal was to travel at least four times a year to various parts of the world. She had it all mapped out: where she would go each year and how long she would stay (on average, two to three weeks at each location). What Lisa did not plan for was what she would be doing when she was not traveling. Despite her busy travel schedule, she spent most of her time at home. She soon realized that retirement was not just about hopping on planes and flying around the world; she needed to develop some objectives for her day-to-day life.

STRUCTURE YOUR TIME

Your first months in retirement will be a learning process to discover how your days will flow. Deciding how to spend your time with no predetermined factor such as work to schedule around is unfamiliar territory. While it is freeing to make your own decisions about how to spend your time, it can also be challenging. You've probably never had so much time on your hands. The key is to spend it on what is important to you. The exercises in this section will help you prioritize your time to meet your short-term goals.

Time Management

An effective time-management technique for retirees is the POSEC method. The acronym stands for Prioritize by Organizing, Streamlining, Economizing, and Contributing. Here's how:

> **P**rioritize your tasks, retirement life goals, and what is important to you.

> **O**rganize your tasks and goals, and plan how to work on them.

> **S**treamline tasks, chores, and all the little things you don't want to do but must.

> **E**conomize what's enjoyable but is low on the priority list.

> **C**ontribute to the community and pay attention to what makes a difference to you.

Identify Your Priorities

Now that you are developing a more detailed plan for your daily retirement life, it's time to prioritize what areas of life are most important to you. This will help you make better decisions about how to spend your time.

As you review this list of nine main life areas, consider their place in your life:

COMMUNITY INVOLVEMENT/VOLUNTEERING

EDUCATION/LEARNING NEW SKILLS

ENTERTAINMENT/TRAVEL

FAMILY

FITNESS (EXERCISE)

FRIENDSHIPS

PURSUIT OF PASSIONS

SPIRITUALITY/RELIGION

WORK/ENTREPRENEURSHIP

There's no need to be confined to this list; feel free to omit some areas and/or add others. Now list the areas in order of their priority to you in your retirement life.

My Priority List

1. _____

_____

2. _____

_____

3. _____

_____

4. _____

_____

5. _____

_____

6. _____

_____

7. _____

_____

8. _____

_____

9. _____

_____

The Focus of Your Short-Term Goals

Now is the time to start putting all your retirement passions and dreams into action. The prompts in this exercise will help you pinpoint a focus for your short-term goals. It's essential to be intentional about achieving your goals, but start small and build from there.

Flip through previous exercises that helped you identify your passions and interests. What one or two passions and/or interests would you like to focus on within the first six months of retirement?

_____

_____

Remember, your "why" is your driving force. Without it, it is easy to lose interest and get distracted. Why is this passion and/or interest important to focus on first?

_____

_____

_____

Are there any obstacles to reaching your goal? If so, how will you overcome them?

_____

_____

_____

What will success look like when you reach your short-term goal?

_____

_____

_____

Develop an Action Plan to Reach Your Goal

Use this table to set a start date and an end date for each specific step you need to take to reach your goal. For example, if your short-term goal is to complete a computer course, your first step may be to research available classes (two days), your next step may be to reach out to a couple of instructors (three days), your third step may be to sign up (one day), and then you'll want to show up, do the coursework, and so on, until you reach your goal.

Being clear on when you will do something and what you need to do by then will keep you motivated and on track. Re-create this table on paper or on the computer for any other short-term goals you might have.

Short-Term Goal: _____

Specific Steps	Start Date	End Date
1.		
2.		
3.		
4.		
5.		

Assess Your Action Plan

As you've seen, most short-term goals require a series of action steps. As you work through your action plan, ask:

	Yes	No
Is this step achievable?		
If not, can I adjust the step to make it achievable?		
Am I giving myself enough time to complete it?		
If not, can I extend the time I need without compromising the goal?		
If I hit an obstacle, can I figure out a way to work around it?		
If not, can I adjust the goal to negate the obstacle?		

If it turns out that one or more of your steps keeps you from actually reaching the goal, identify the lessons learned. Keep them in mind when setting new short-term goals by noting them here:

_____

_____

_____

_____

_____

_____

A DAY IN THE LIFE

How you spend your days results in how you spend your years. What will your typical day look like in retirement? Will your days be structured, free-flowing, or a combination of both? If you plan to wing it, you may find that, over time, you become bored and restless. Having a rhythm to your retirement day helps you stay organized, active, and social. The key is to structure your days with the intention of meeting the retirement lifestyle you have envisioned. The exercises in this section will help you build your daily flow.

One Step Beyond

What will you do with all your free time? You already have some general ideas of what to do—but have you thought about adding a stretch goal to those activities? Consider the following:

Take an exercise class ➡ Run a short marathon

Work part time ➡ Build a business

Play sports ➡ Join a competitive league

Pick up a new hobby ➡ Sell what you make

Read ➡ Write your memoirs

Mentor someone ➡ Start a tutoring business

What's Your Preference?

To get a general idea of how best to organize your average day, begin by considering your preferences. On a scale of 1 to 10, with 1 being not at all, 5 being neutral, and 10 being very much, rate each of the following statements.

I like to have a set routine to follow.

1   2   3   4   5   6   7   8   9   10

It is important to me to work toward accomplishing something daily/weekly.

1   2   3   4   5   6   7   8   9   10

I get bored if I'm not busy.

1   2   3   4   5   6   7   8   9   10

Socializing during the week is important to me.

1   2   3   4   5   6   7   8   9   10

I like to have considerable alone time throughout the day.

1   2   3   4   5   6   7   8   9   10

I like to be spontaneous.

1   2   3   4   5   6   7   8   9   10

Look at any statement you rated 6 or above. Be sure that when structuring your average day in retirement, you take your strongest preferences into consideration.

Your New Morning Routine

When you are newly retired, one of the most noticeable changes is your morning routine. Think about all the weekday mornings you spent getting ready for work. You are probably feeling grateful you no longer have to rush out the door. It's still a good idea, however, to develop a morning routine to help set the tone for your day.

What time would you like to wake up? _____

What time would you like to have breakfast? _____

What time would you like to get washed and dressed? _____

List three positive activities you can incorporate into your new morning routine (for example, exercising, reading, meditating, journaling):

1. _____

2. _____

3. _____

Your New Daytime Routine

It's great to have more time to do things that you enjoy throughout the day. Think about the activities/tasks you want to incorporate into your everyday life.

List three activities or tasks you would like to do routinely during the day:

1. _____

2. _____

3. _____

List three activities or tasks you would like to do occasionally during the day:

1. _____

2. _____

3. _____

List three activities or tasks you would like to do specifically on weekends:

1. _____

2. _____

3. _____

Your New Evening Routine

Evenings are no longer the time you spend unwinding from the workday and resting up for the next one. There's no longer a need to fit in everything you want to do, and you can make your evenings as leisurely or as busy as you'd like.

What time would you like to have dinner? _____

What time would you like to put on your sleepwear? _____

What time would you like to get into bed? _____

List three positive activities you can incorporate into your new evening routine:

1. _____

2. _____

3. _____

Create an Ideal Week

If you had the perfect retirement week, what would it look like? How would you spend your days? What would you be doing? Who would you be socializing with? What activities would you be doing? Would you be pursuing your passions and goals? Would much of your time be spent relaxing?

Remember, how you spend your days in retirement is how you will spend your life in retirement. Fill out this table to envision your perfect week, one that makes you feel fulfilled. Think about your passions, what you are curious about, and how your curiosity can be incorporated into your daily life. This will allow you to become intentional about planning out your days to live the retirement life you dreamed about.

Day	My Ideal Retirement Week
Sunday	Morning:
	Afternoon:
	Evening:
Monday	Morning:
	Afternoon:
	Evening:

Day	My Ideal Retirement Week
Tuesday	Morning:
	Afternoon:
	Evening:
Wednesday	Morning:
	Afternoon:
	Evening:
Thursday	Morning:
	Afternoon:
	Evening:
Friday	Morning:
	Afternoon:
	Evening:
Saturday	Morning:
	Afternoon:
	Evening:

CREATE NEW HABITS

You likely developed habits that became a routine part of your working life without even realizing it. Maybe during your free time, you watched TV. Subconsciously, you made the association that free time equals TV time. This habit may have helped you relax after work, but in retirement, you don't want to spend all your free time watching TV. Now that you are retired, make sure your habits inspire you. If they don't, create new habits that will help you have a fulfilling life. The exercises in this section will help you break bad habits and create positive ones.

New-Habit Tips

Creating a new habit takes time and patience. Here are important things to keep in mind to help you along your way:

> Stick to the habit as often as you can until it becomes second nature.

> Be flexible. Step away and give yourself time to refocus if necessary.

> Pair the new habit with something you enjoy (for example, listening listen to your favorite music during exercise).

> Focus on the big-picture outcome when the habit becomes your usual behavior.

> Plan a celebration when the new practice becomes part of your routine.

Habits to Break

With more time on your hands, you will want to start noticing how you spend most of your downtime. These may have been habits you picked up over the years to wind down from work. If they aren't aligned with your values and the life you want to live, list them in this table and explore why you want to break the habits (remember, your "why" is your motivation) and the impact this will have on your life.

Habit to Break	Why You Want to Break This Habit	The Benefit of Breaking the Habit

Set Goals to Break the Habit

To break your habit, start with daily goals to limit the amount of time you engage in it. For example, if you feel that you are watching too much TV or spending too much time playing a game on your phone, you could start with a daily practice of turning off the television or stopping the game after a certain amount of time. If you feel that you snack too much, you could limit yourself to one or two pieces or eat something healthy instead.

Habit to Break	Daily Goal to Break the Habit

Create New Habits

There are undoubtedly many new things you want to do. Some of them will be new habits you want to create to live a more successful and fulfilling retirement. Creating new habits can be challenging because it requires you to be intentional about what you do. Knowing why you want to create the habit and what small actions you can take makes it a little easier.

New Habit	Why You Want to Start This Habit	Daily Action to Create the New Habit

Trigger the New Habit

Habits are usually triggered by something. So if you want to adopt a new habit, tie it to a trigger. For habits to stick, you must train your mind. For example, if you want to walk 30 minutes in the morning, put your walking shoes by your bed at night. When you wake up in the morning, seeing your walking shoes reminds you of the walk. For each new habit you want to start, think of something that will trigger it.

New Habit	Habit Trigger

Habits to Help You Reach Your Goals

Creating positive habits can make a remarkable difference, with the ultimate goal being a happy and fulfilling life in retirement. Think again about your short-term goals and aspirations. What daily, weekly, and monthly habits can help you reach your goals?

In this table, list a few short-term goals. Identify what actions and behaviors would help you reach them.

Short-Term Goal	Helpful Habits

Find an Accountability Partner

An accountability partner can help you stay on track as you build new habits. For example, if your goal is to exercise more, ask a friend to join you at the gym, hire a personal trainer, or join a group exercise class. If you want to spend more time reading, your accountability partner can read the same book or ask you about it at set intervals. Having a support system is an excellent way to help you stick with your goal to create a new habit.

Complete this table for each new habit that could benefit from an accountability partner. Identify what that person's task would be to hold you accountable.

New Habit	Accountability Partner's Role

For each role you identified, who would be a good accountability partner and why?

Chapter 7

LONG-TERM GOALS

When you reach the end of your first year of retirement, what do you want to have accomplished? What about the years beyond that? What do they look like? As you embark upon this new phase of your life, start mapping out your plans for reaching your goals a year or more from now. The passions and interests you have identified so far are probably not spur-of-the-moment desires, but things you wish to be doing for years to come.

For me, starting a coaching business was one of my long-term goals in retirement. After a couple of months of decompressing from work, which included resting and traveling, I began focusing on my goal of starting my business. For me, this meant blocking off some time on certain days to work on it. I did a lot of research and talked to people in the industry. I also practiced coaching with friends to see whether this was something I wanted to pursue. By the end of the year, I had developed a business plan that kept me on track. A long-term goal doesn't have to be starting a business, of course. Your long-term goals can take the form of anything that is meaningful to you.

CREATE AN ACTION PLAN

Your first year of retirement is full of anticipation and possibilities. You've thought about your goals and dreamed about how this first year will look; however, dreams are just dreams until you make them happen. It's time to focus on creating an action plan for your retirement goals. What are the first steps you'll take? Remember to allow for flexibility; this is a new lifestyle with much uncertainty. The exercises in this section will get you started living the fun, exciting, and restful retirement life you envision.

The Phases of Retirement

It's normal to experience a gamut of emotions when you are newly retired. It isn't always a smooth transition. It helps to be aware of the retirement phases people generally go through, along with the associated feelings, so you can know what to expect.

> **Honeymoon:** The beginning of your retirement. You are relaxing, planning trips, and reconnecting with family and friends, and you may not be putting much thought into what is next.

> **Disenchantment:** The honeymoon is over and you start asking yourself, "What's next?"

> **Reorientation:** You are ready to get out there and learn new things. You start creating goals.

> **Stability:** You begin to find your groove that leads to your happily-ever-after.

Set Long-Term Goals

Long-term goals take a year or more to accomplish. It's possible that some of your short-term goals are steps toward your long-term goals, or maybe your long-term goals are independent of anything you've done before. Long-term goals might be something like scanning and organizing the five decades' worth of photo albums in your parents' closet, starting a new business or nonprofit, or moving your residence.

List three goals that will take a year or more to accomplish:

Goal 1:

Goal 2:

Goal 3:

For each goal, explain why it is important to you:

Goal 1:

Goal 2:

Goal 3:

Which of your values is associated with each goal?

Goal 1:

Goal 2:

Goal 3:

Fine-Tune Your Long-Term Goals

Hopefully your long-term goals match your values, but some may not. You may need to fine-tune your goals to bring them into alignment with your values. If this is the case, answer the questions below to help you define and reach your goals.

If your goals are aligned with your values, what actions do you need to take to bring them into alignment?

_____

_____

_____

_____

Are there any obstacles to meeting your goals? If so, how will you address them?

_____

_____

_____

_____

Describe how success would look if you accomplished your goals:

_____

_____

_____

_____

Map Out Your Long-Term Goal

As you think about your long-term goals, focus on the actions you need to take to accomplish them. Because long-term goals take time, it's important to have a plan. When you map them out, start with your goal as your central point. Next, think of the actions that are needed to accomplish it.

Based on the actions, what steps will you need to take? For example, your *goal* may be to start a part-time business. An *action* may be to research the business. Your *steps* may be to read books on the business, attend workshops/classes, and listen to an expert's podcast. Use this diagram to help you map out your first goal.

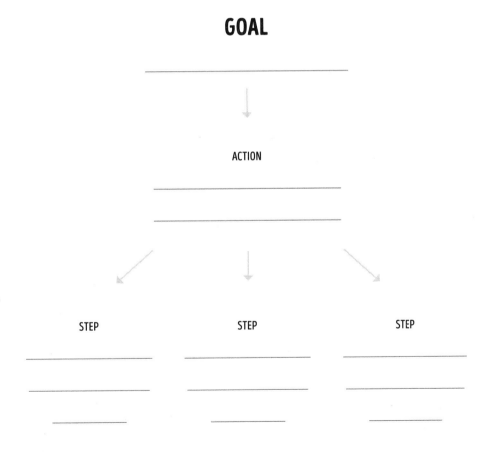

GOAL

ACTION

STEP   STEP   STEP

Plan Milestone Celebrations

Retirement is about enjoying life to the fullest, and part of enjoying life is celebrating. As you reach milestones, big or small, in pursuing your goals, be sure to celebrate! This inspires you to keep going and is a great confidence booster. Create some milestones to celebrate as you pursue your long-term goals, and brainstorm ways to acknowledge your efforts.

Milestone	Celebration Ideas

Try Time Blocking

There may be specific tasks you want to complete, but you find that nothing is getting done. It's possible that you're getting distracted or that you aren't setting aside enough time to take care of the tasks that will bring you closer to your goals.

Time blocking can help you structure your day to get things done to incrementally reach your goals. Use the time-blocking table on the next two pages to identify the day(s) and hour(s) you will dedicate to working on your tasks. When you commit to spending this time working toward your goals, you will start to see them take shape.

	Sunday	Monday	Tuesday
AM			
6:00			
7:00			
8:00			
9:00			
10:00			
11:00			
PM			
12:00			
1:00			
2:00			
3:00			
4:00			
5:00			
6:00			
7:00			
8:00			
9:00			
10:00			
11:00			

Wednesday	Thursday	Friday	Saturday

KEEP CALM AND CARRY ON

You have spent a lot of time exploring who you are and what is important to you in retirement. Now let's shift your focus to other essential areas for a happy retirement, such as nurturing yourself, staying healthy, and feeling grounded. As you continue your retirement journey, you will want to ensure that you are living a balanced lifestyle. Harmony in your life will lead to happiness, and the exercises in this section will guide you forward.

Take a Breather

Not every minute of your retirement day needs to be packed with something to do. You have worked all these years, so let yourself take a breather. Here are some benefits of doing nothing:

> Your mind and body have a chance to rest.

> You can focus better later because your mind is clear.

> You feel recharged and rested.

> Stress and anxiety are lowered.

Doing nothing doesn't have to literally mean nothing. Perhaps you will listen to soothing music, focus on your breathing, visualize being somewhere relaxing, or take a stroll in nature.

Step Off the Treadmill

When you were working, it may have felt like you were going all the time. You tried to squeeze in some "me time" when you could, but it was usually not enough. As a newly retired person, you may be so used to that treadmill that you just don't know how to get off. Retirement is the time to bring more balance to your life, so start thinking about what you like to do during your "me time."

Name something that brings you comfort (taking a hot bath or nature walk, lighting a scented candle):

_____

Name something that helps you relax (reading, painting, listening to music):

_____

Name something that makes you feel special (getting a spa treatment, treating yourself to a delicacy):

_____

Name something fun you like to do (play a sport, socialize):

_____

Brainstorm ways to incorporate these activities into your retirement lifestyle here:

_____

_____

_____

_____

Gauge Your Health Plan

Maintaining a healthy lifestyle in retirement is vital—your health is your wealth. Gauge your overall health plan in the following areas.

I visit my doctor routinely for wellness checkups.

Always   Generally   Occasionally   Never

Based on your response, do you need to improve? If yes, what steps will you take?

_____

_____

I eat a healthy diet.

Always   Generally   Occasionally   Never

Based on your response, do you need to improve? If yes, what steps will you take?

_____

_____

I do exercises that challenge my strength and balance.

Always   Generally   Occasionally   Never

Based on your response, do you need to improve? If yes, what steps will you take?

_____

_____

I get a restful sleep at night.

Always   Generally   Occasionally   Never

Based on your response, do you need to improve? If yes, what steps will you take?

_____

_____

I can manage my stress.

Always   Generally   Occasionally   Never

Based on your response, do you need to improve? If yes, what steps will you take?

_____

_____

I do stimulating activities (like learning new skills) that challenge my brain.

Always   Generally   Occasionally   Never

Based on your response, do you need to improve? If yes, what steps will you take?

_____

_____

Schedule Physical Activity and Exercise

Throughout life, exercise helps us maintain a strong and healthy body, but as we age, it becomes essential for staying mobile and flexible. Caring for your physical body is critical for feeling good and happy throughout your retirement years. So start off with your long-term health in mind and have an exercise plan.

In this table, jot down all the physical activities and exercises you will engage in. Note the frequency and the length of time you will dedicate to them. Think of a variety of activities and exercises you enjoy that will keep you inspired to maintain the routine.

Exercise/Activity	Frequency	Length of Time

Set Aside Time for Spiritual Connection

If spirituality/religion is important to you, be sure to incorporate it into your retirement lifestyle. Many retirees find they want a deeper connection with their spiritual or religious beliefs, while some choose to explore other faiths. If this area is important to you, find a way to fit it into your life.

If you plan to attend religious and/or spiritual gatherings or services, note the days and times they meet so you can put them on your calendar:

_____

_____

If you plan to create your own religious and/or spiritual rituals, describe them:

_____

_____

_____

_____

If you are interested in exploring other beliefs or faiths, describe what interests you and the exploration steps involved:

_____

_____

_____

Conclusion
LOOKING AHEAD

Congratulations! You have put a lot of effort into planning for this first year of your retirement and beyond. I hope the exercises and tips have helped you build the foundation of a fantastic retirement future, one in which you feel inspired to live fully. While you may encounter twists and turns along your journey, always be intentional about working toward your goals and interests. Frequently review your values and ensure that they align with your retirement vision.

As you continue to grow and flourish in retirement, refer to this workbook whenever you need help with other projects, experiences, or situations you may not have addressed initially. It is always available to guide you throughout the years ahead.

Finally, enjoy retirement. There is no one-size-fits-all approach to a happy retirement. It is what you make it. You have worked hard to develop a plan to help guide you; now execute it and have some fun. Don't hold back! Now is the time to go full-throttle ahead.

Appendix
RETIREMENT VISION BOARD

It would be difficult to summarize all the work you have done in this workbook on one page. This vison board gives you a quick overview of your hopes and dreams for a fulfilling retirement. Fill it in based on your responses to the workbook exercises. This represents only a snippet of your retirement life, but I hope it inspires you to see what a wonderful future you have planned.

Retirement Motto

_____

TOP 3 VALUES

_____

_____

_____

DAILY LIFE IN RETIREMENT

_____

_____

_____

_____

_____

#1 GOAL/ASPIRATION

_____

RETIREMENT ANNUAL INCOME

$ _____

INNER CIRCLE
FAMILY & FRIENDS

_____

_____

_____

_____

HOBBIES/INTERESTS

_____

_____

_____

_____

RESOURCES

BOOKS

The Retirement Challenge: A Non-financial Guide from Top Retirement Experts by Retirement Coaches Association Members—A thought-provoking book written by retirement experts covering various nonfinancial retirement topics.

Tiny Habits: The Small Changes That Change Everything by BJ Fogg, PhD— A step-by-step guide to help you create new habits and stick to them.

The Ultimate Retirement Guide for 50+: Winning Strategies to Make Your Money Last a Lifetime by Suze Orman—Practical financial advice to help you plan for retirement in today's changing landscape.

Your 168: Finding Purpose and Satisfaction in a Value-Based Life by Harry M. Jansen Kraemer, Jr.—Learn how to pursue a valued-based life by identifying and committing to your values and priorities.

WEBSITES

AARP.org—A vast library of retirement resources, calculators, and articles.

Bankrate.com—This site offers information and various retirement calculators to help you plan for retirement.

GlobalVolunteers.org—International volunteer programs that offer experiences of a lifetime.

NextAvenue.org—Their mission is to provide reliable information to help individuals age 50+ figure out what's next in work, finance, health, and lifestyle.

SeniorMatch.com—A relationship and dating website for seniors.

PODCASTS

The Retirement Answer Man—Roger Whitney, a certified financial planner, discusses how to plan for a retirement that meets your lifestyle financially.

The Retirement Wisdom Podcast—Host Joe Casey covers various retirement topics with guests offering insights on how to retire successfully.

Second Act Stories—Each episode focuses on individuals pursuing a more rewarding life in their second act.

ACKNOWLEDGMENTS

I am deeply grateful to Zeitgeist for giving me the opportunity to write this retirement workbook. I never imagined I would be an author, but here I am with my first book. A huge thank-you to my editor, Susan Randol. Your patience and understanding throughout this process have been nothing but exceptional. I have learned so much from you.

To my husband, thanks for your support, love, patience, and encouragement. You have always been my rock. To my son, thanks for all your love and inspiration.

I am honored to share my experience and knowledge about retirement planning.

ABOUT THE AUTHOR

Veronica McCain is a Certified Professional Retirement Coach and a Chartered Retirement Planning Counselor. After 31 years of public service work, Veronica retired and dreamed of starting a business to help people through retirement. She founded Savvy Retirement Coach with the mission to provide a holistic retirement planning concept focused on self, health, and wealth. She has worked one-on-one with clients to help them map out a retirement lifestyle specific to their needs. She also conducts interactive retirement events and retreats that bring a unique experience to retirement planning. Veronica's passion in life is to help others reach their dreams. Learn more at savvyretirementcoach.com.